Floral Mandala Art

A Coloring Book for Grown Ups

Relax, Unwind, and Create Beautiful Art

Intricate Flower Inspired Coloring Pages
For Hobby Artists & Crafters

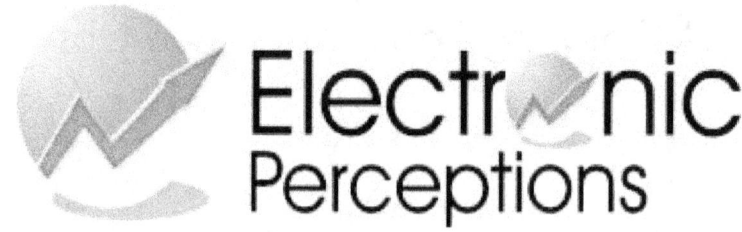

Electronic Perceptions
Tucson, Arizona
www.ElectronicPerceptions.com
©2015 ELECTRONIC PERCEPTIONS, All Rights Reserved

ISBN-13: 978-0985475673 (Electronic Perceptions)
ISBN-10: 0985475676

Custom Artwork by Commissioned Artists.

A Mandala can be super simple or extremely complex, but the end result is always symmetrical and balanced. Symmetry creates feelings of calm, balance, and that everything is right in the world.

For most of us, communing with nature also provides a measure of quiet, calm pleasure that we may not take time for often enough. That's why this book series was developed. Through it and future volumes to come, you can experience renewed levels of relaxation, calm and balance in your world.

Coloring is an easy way to unleash your inner creativity without feeling pressured to be some awesome artist. Instead, you get to grab pencils or crayons, and enjoy a small taste of the simplicity of childhood.

This book contains 25 intricate designs that combine the beauty of floral elements with the balance of the meditative mandala. Each page is blank on the back except for a small page number at the bottom. There is also space beneath each picture so that you may add a custom title, quote of the day, or personal reminisces of what was on your mind while coloring. This is a wonderful way to create a personal journal.

The designs were made with adults in mind and may absorb your attention for several hours if you so choose. They will be adored by older teenagers and creative-minded college students as well.

Use colored pencils, crayons, gel pens, markers or even paint to create artwork worthy of framing in your home. Place a blank piece of thin cardboard, poster board or construction paper behind the image as you're coloring to prevent the colors bleeding onto the next image.

To maximize the stress relieving effects of coloring, turn off the TV, disconnect the Internet, and silence your phone.

Enjoy!

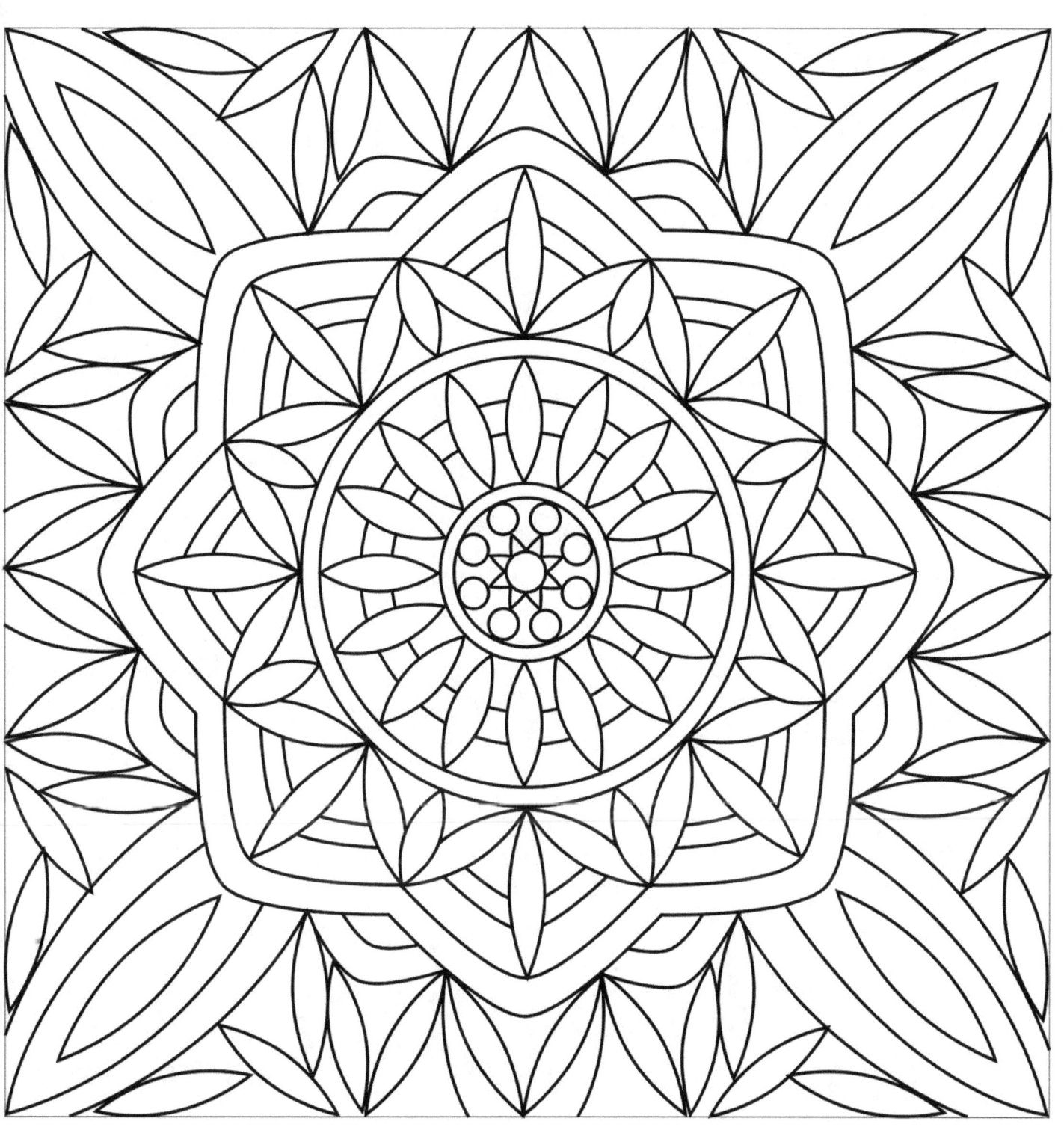

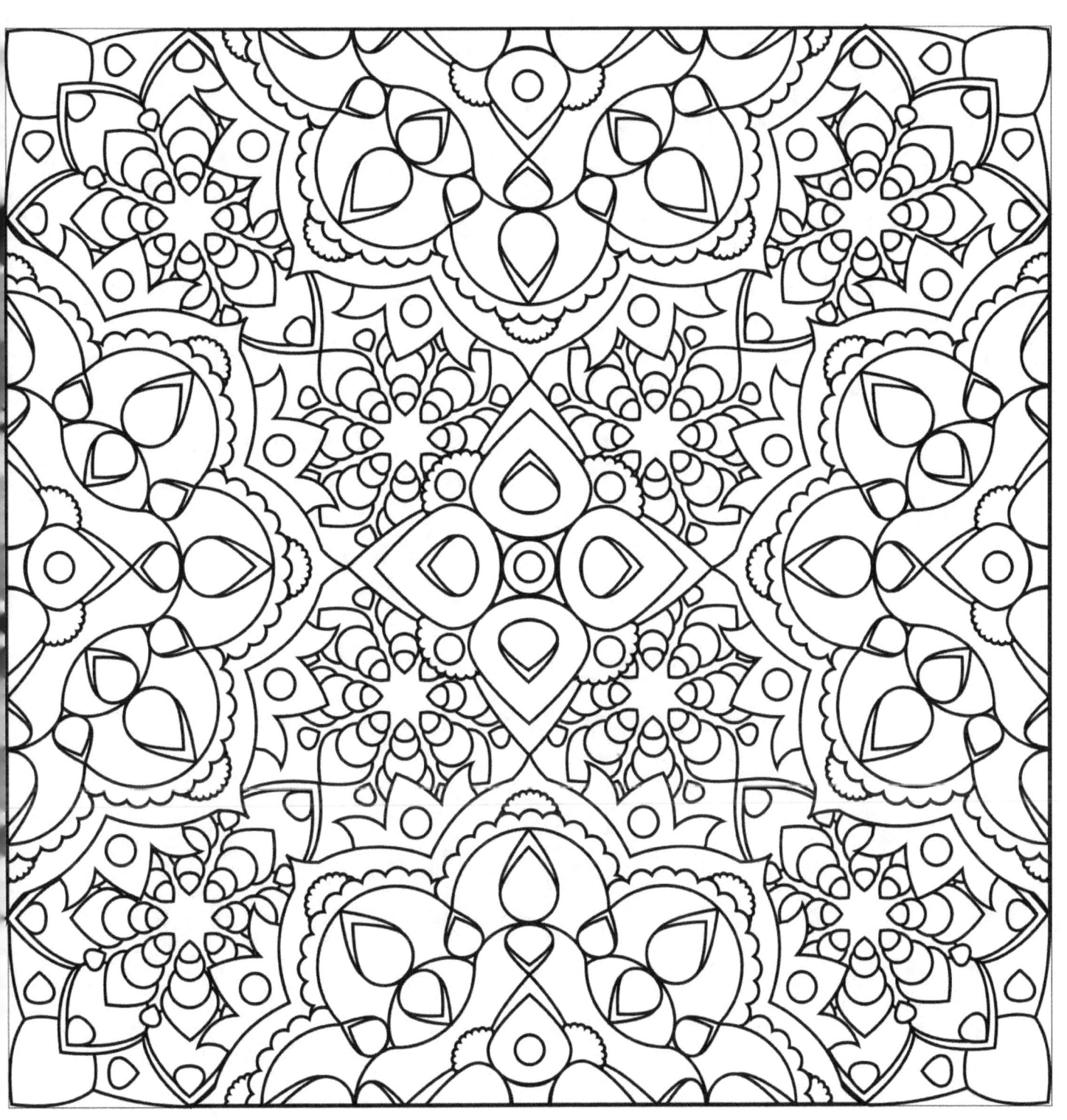

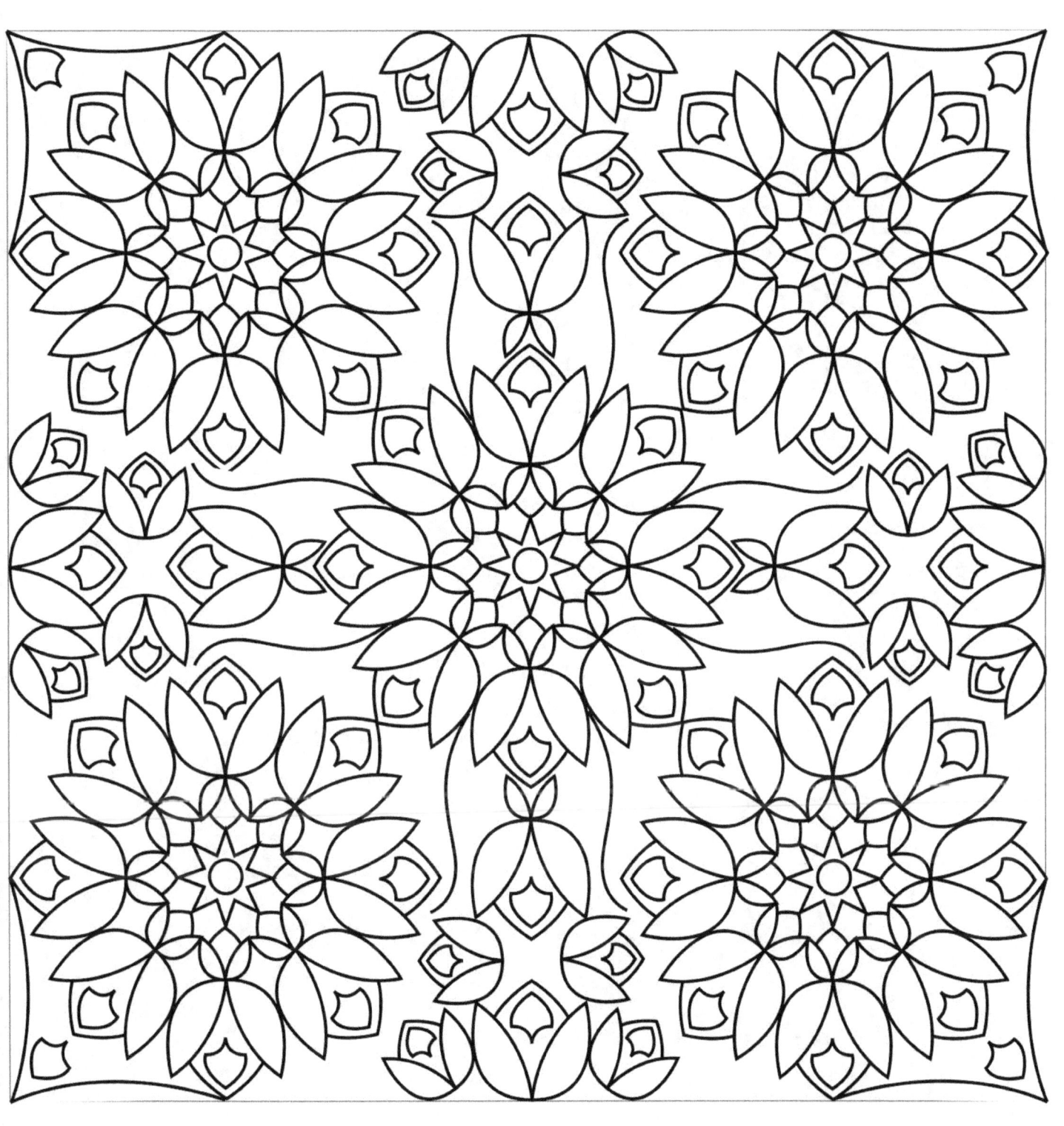

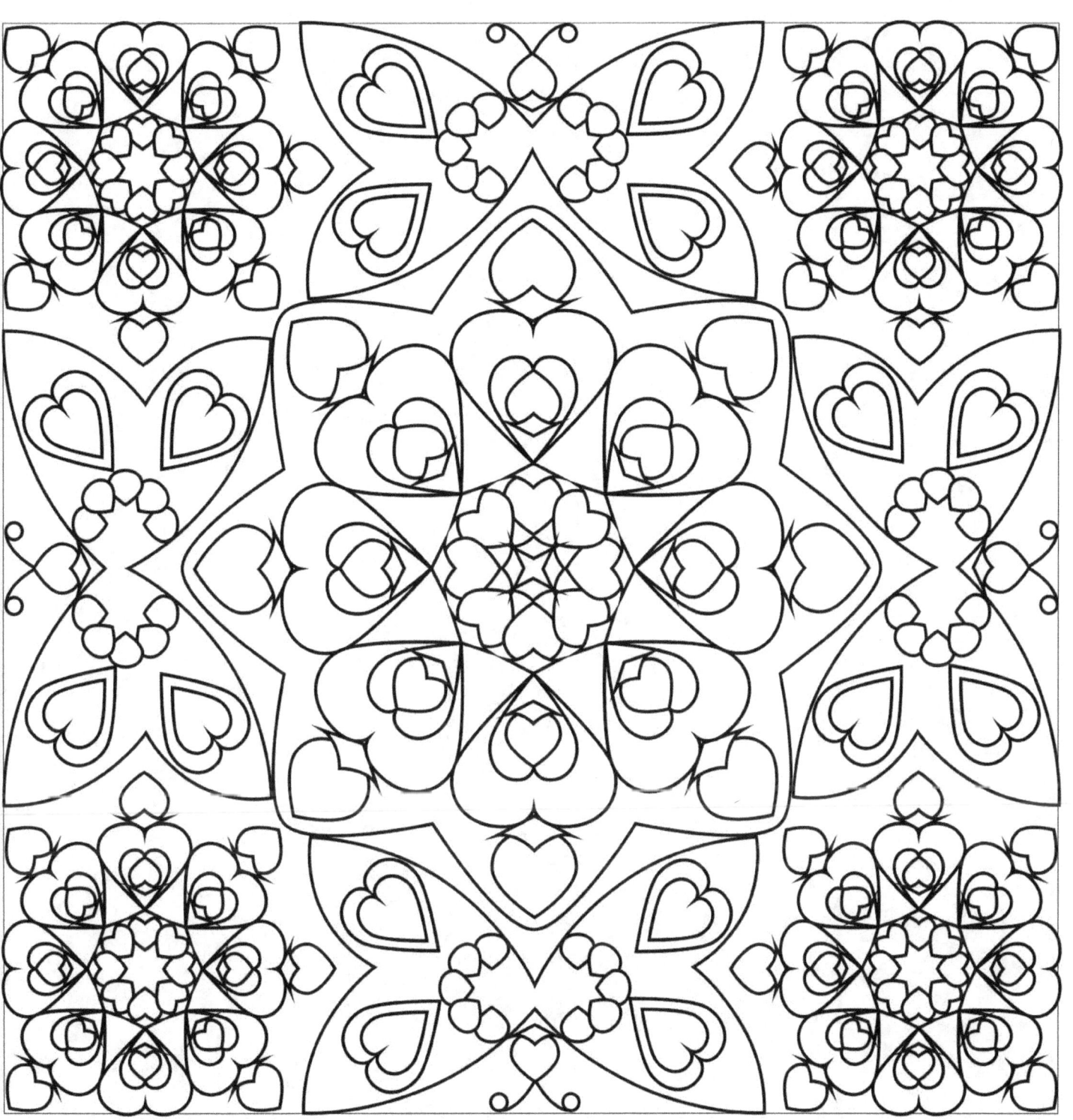

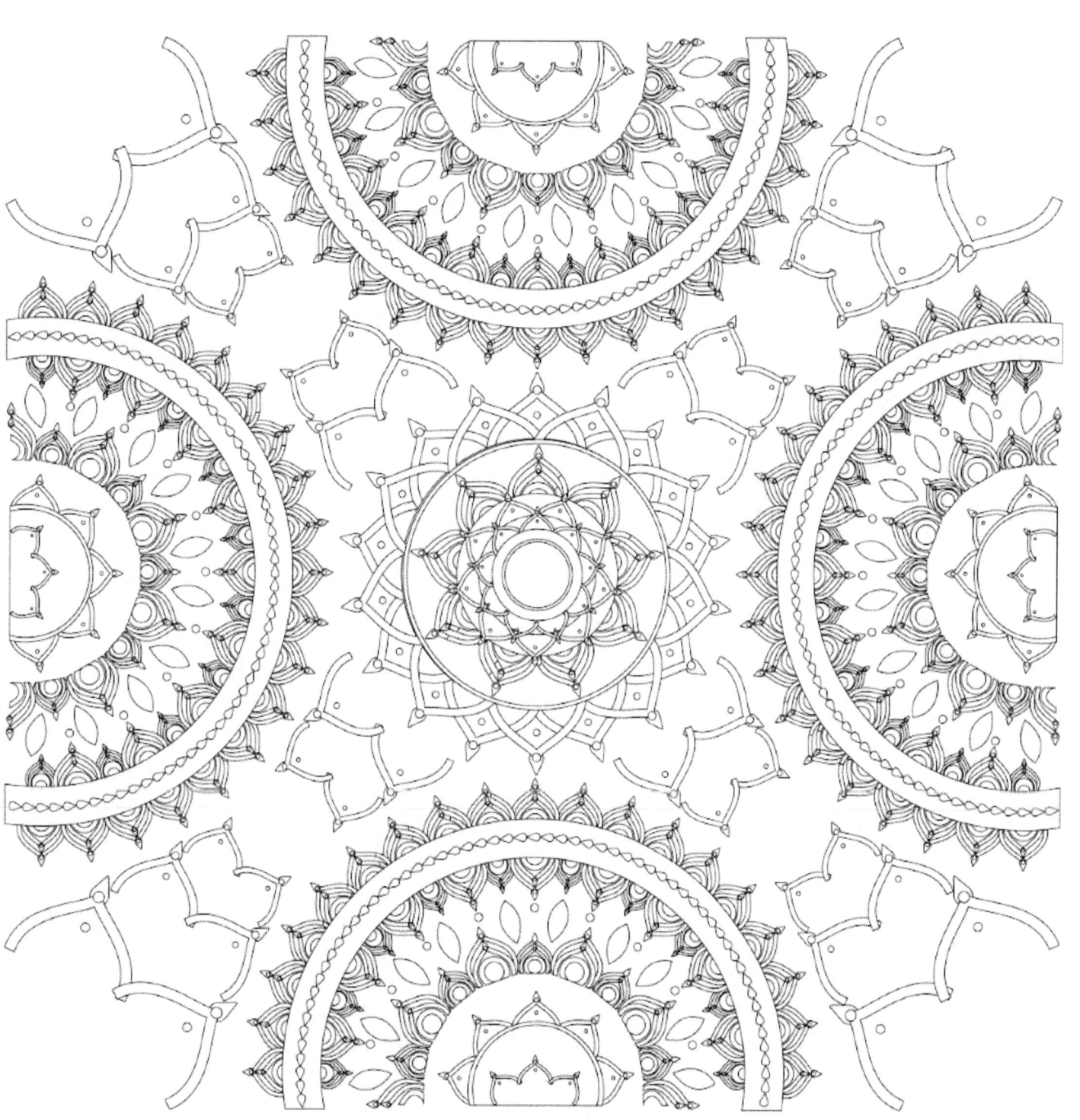

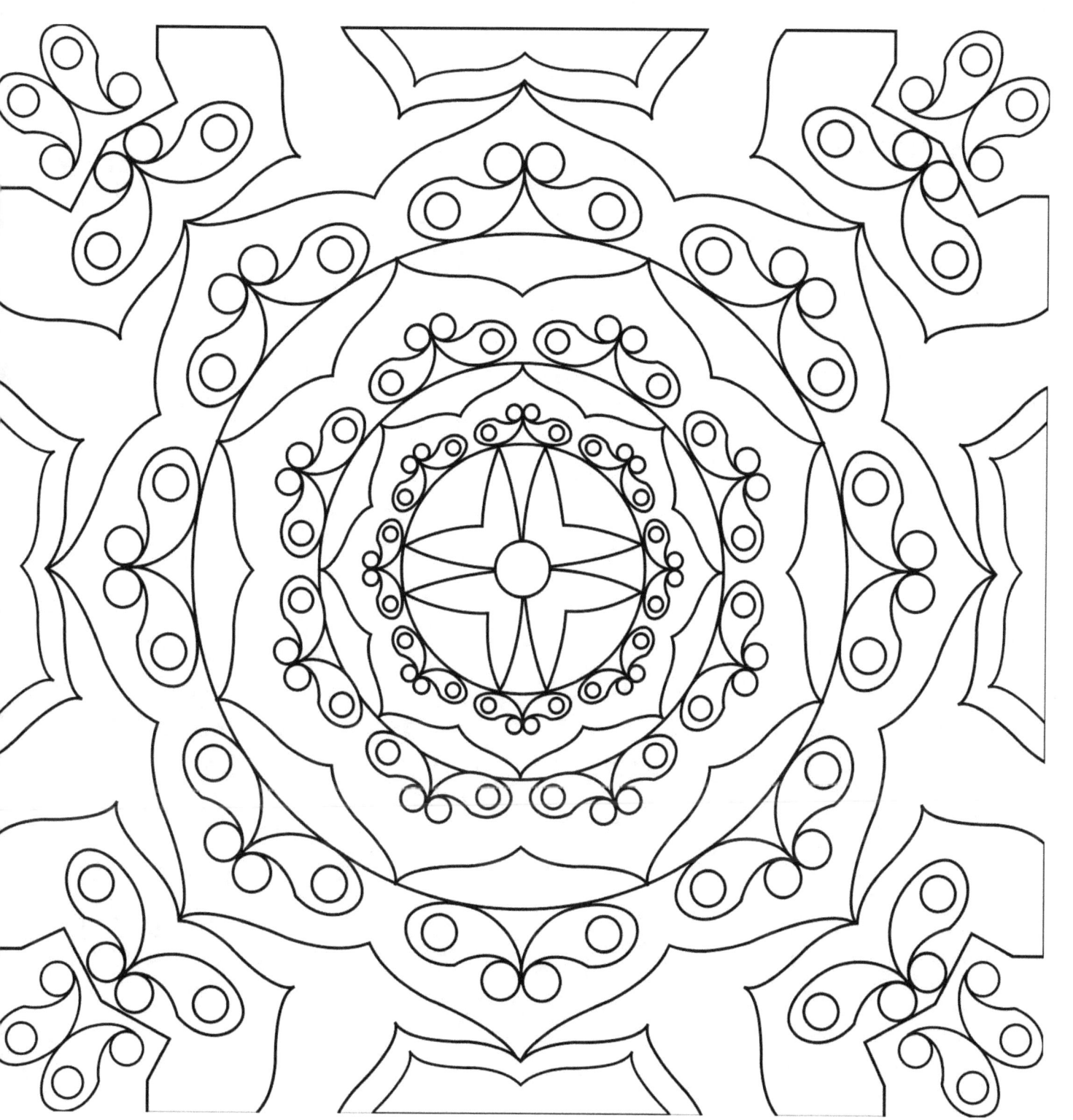

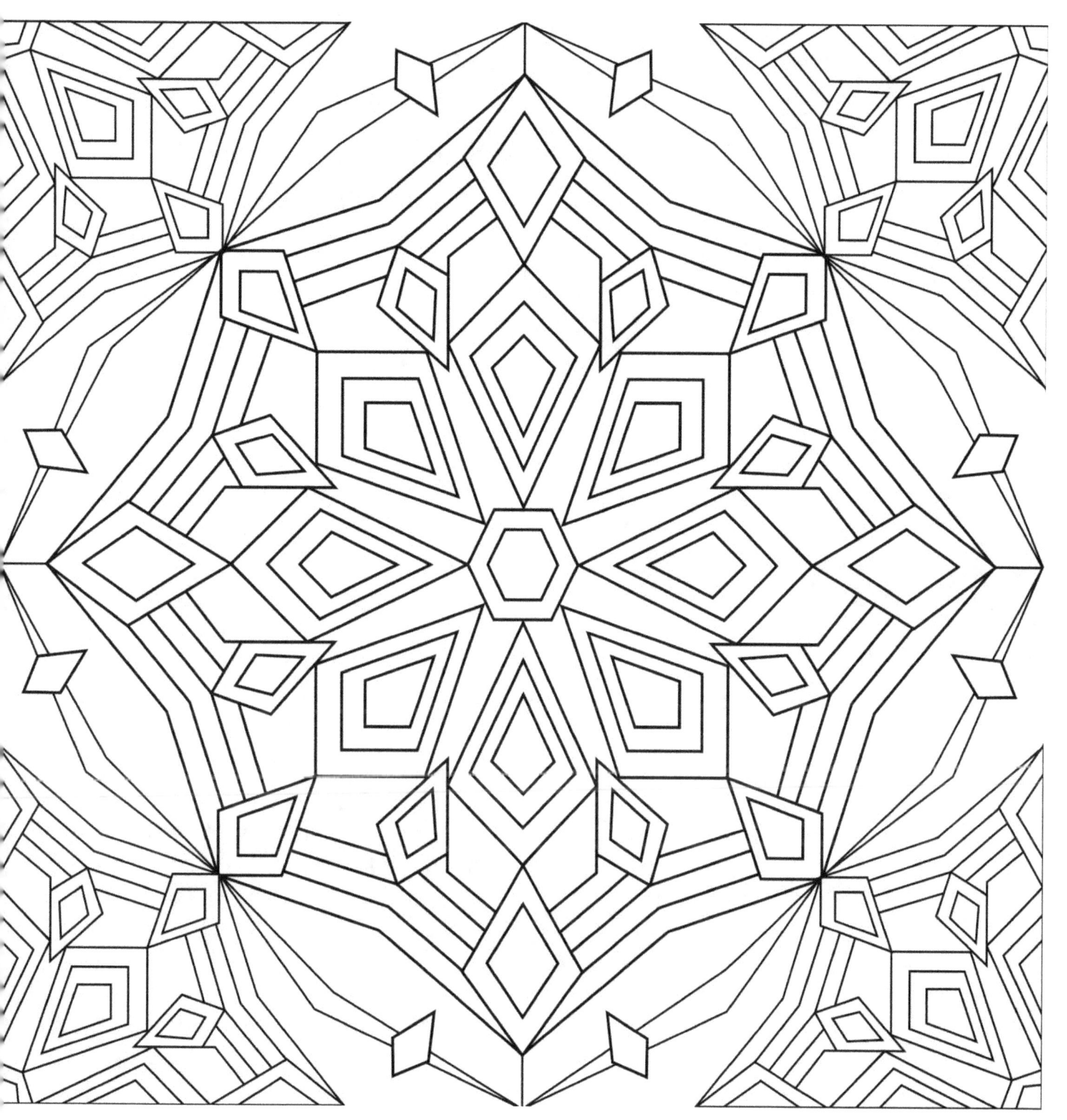

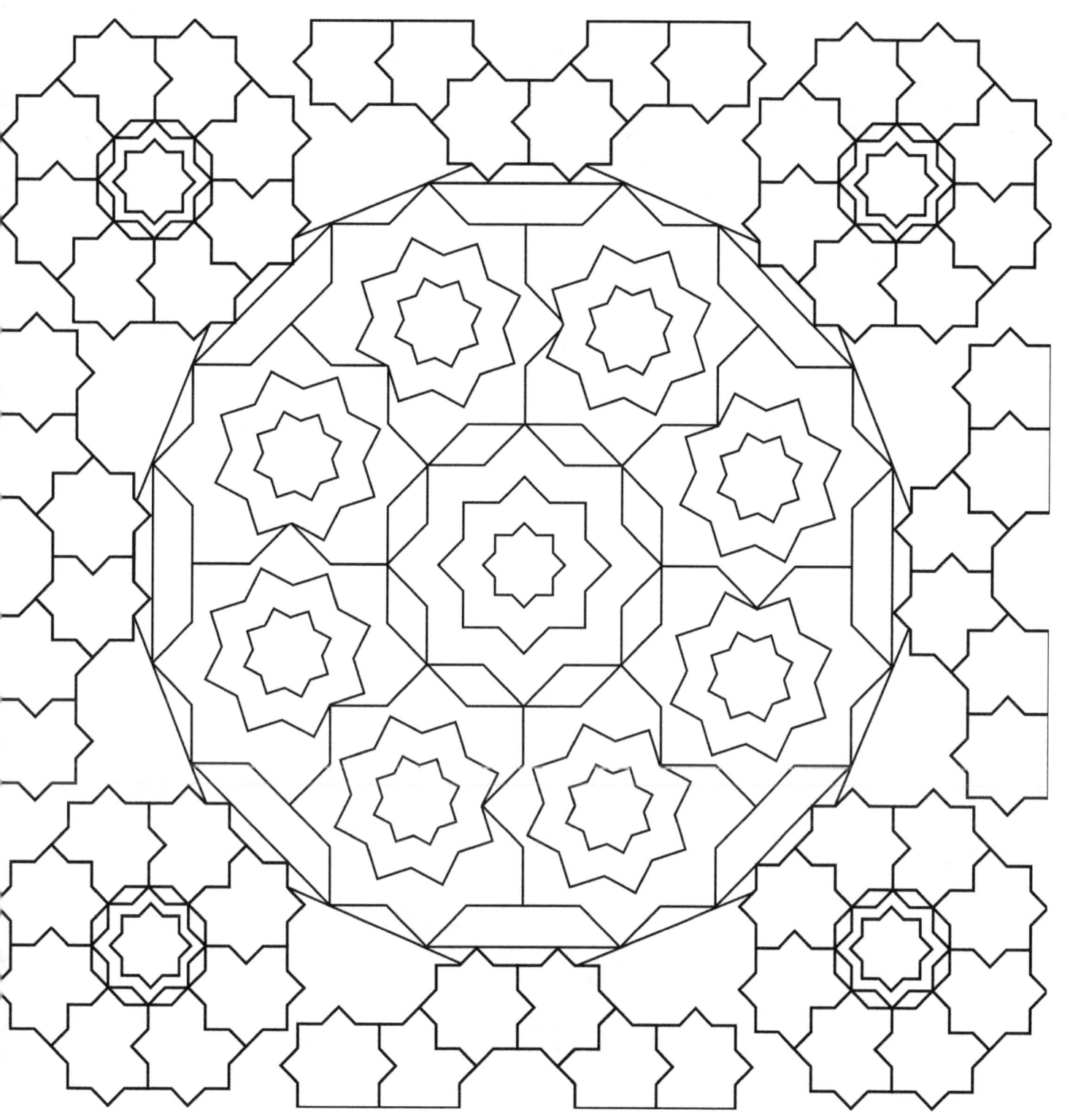

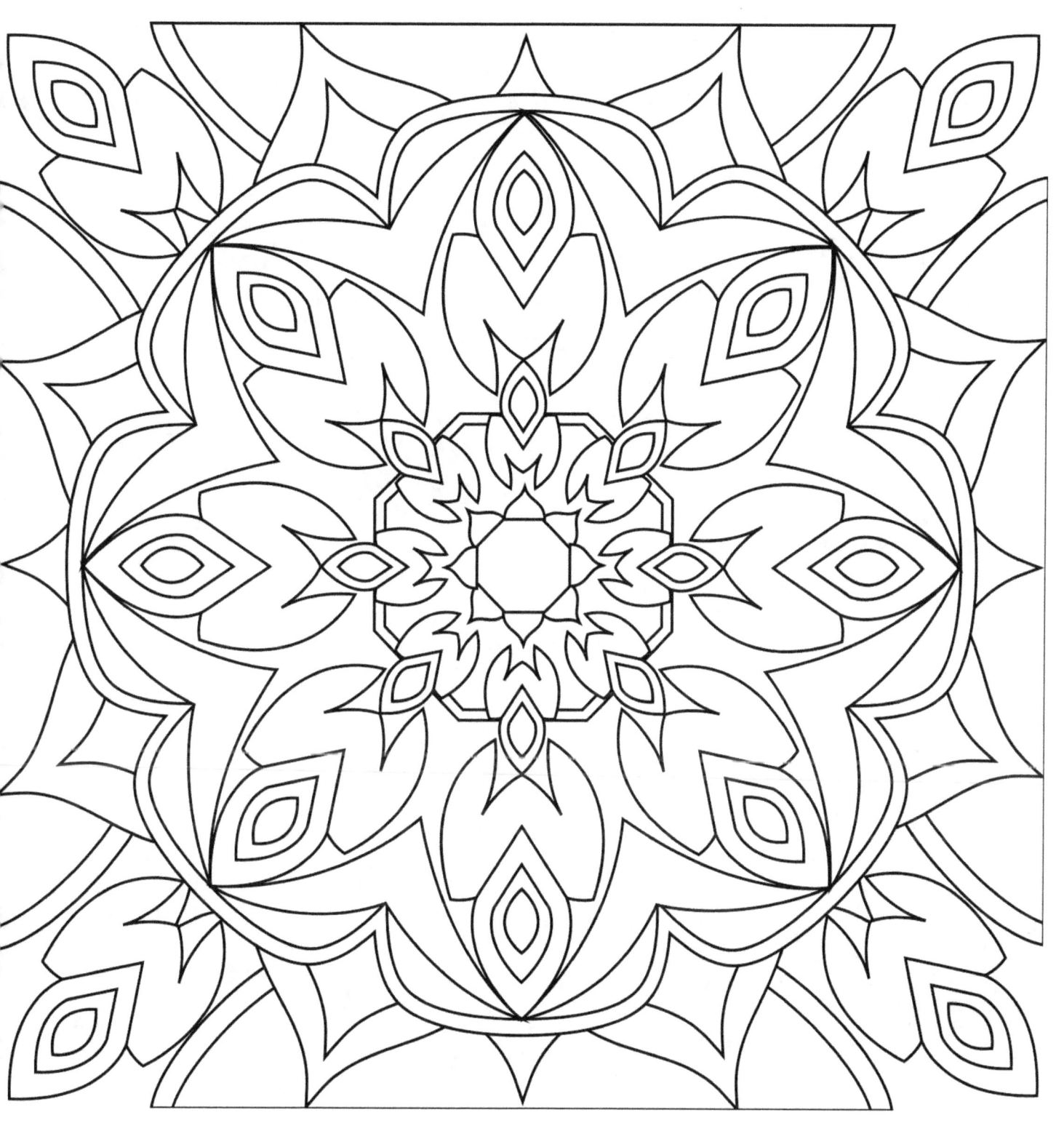

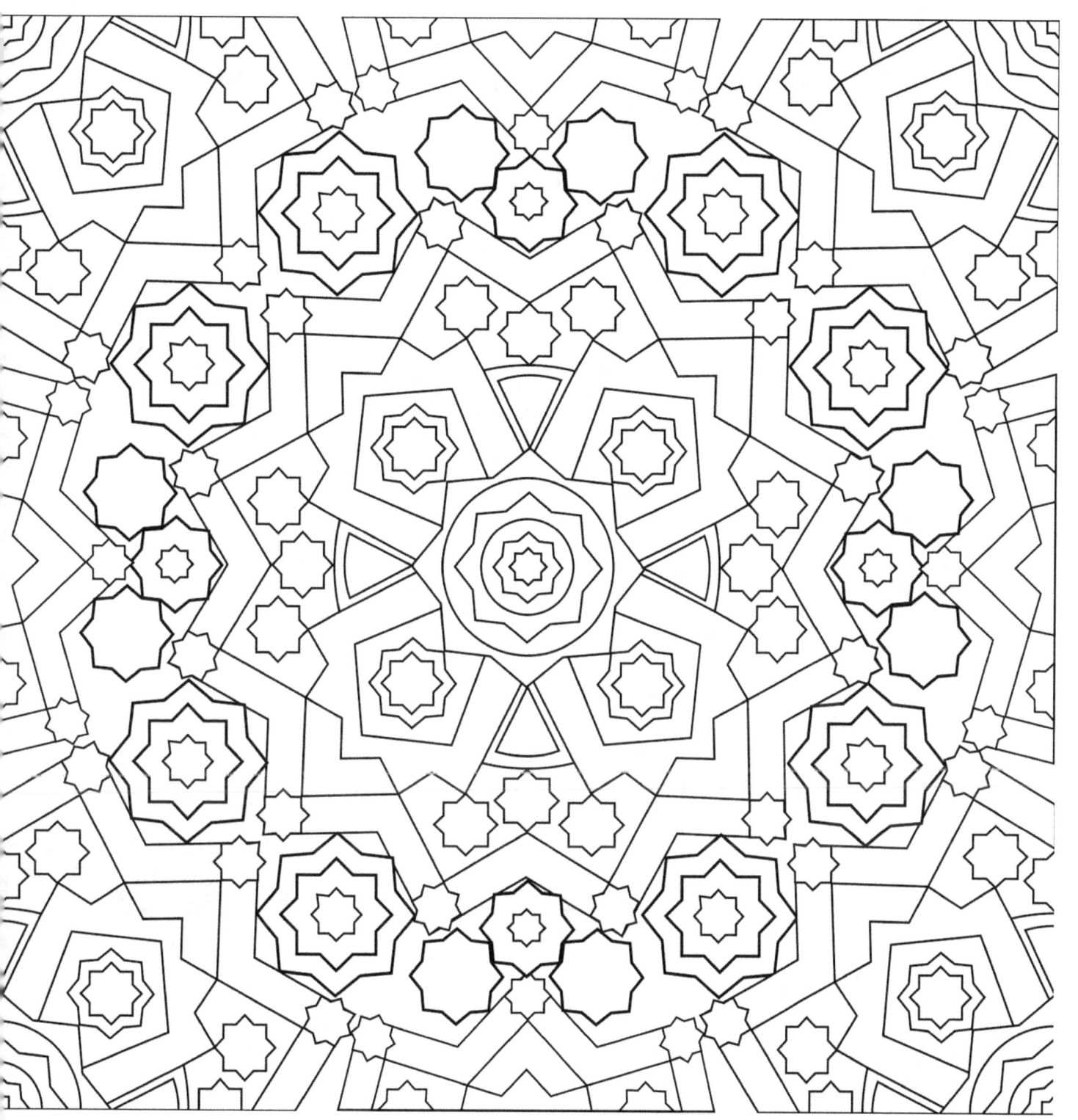

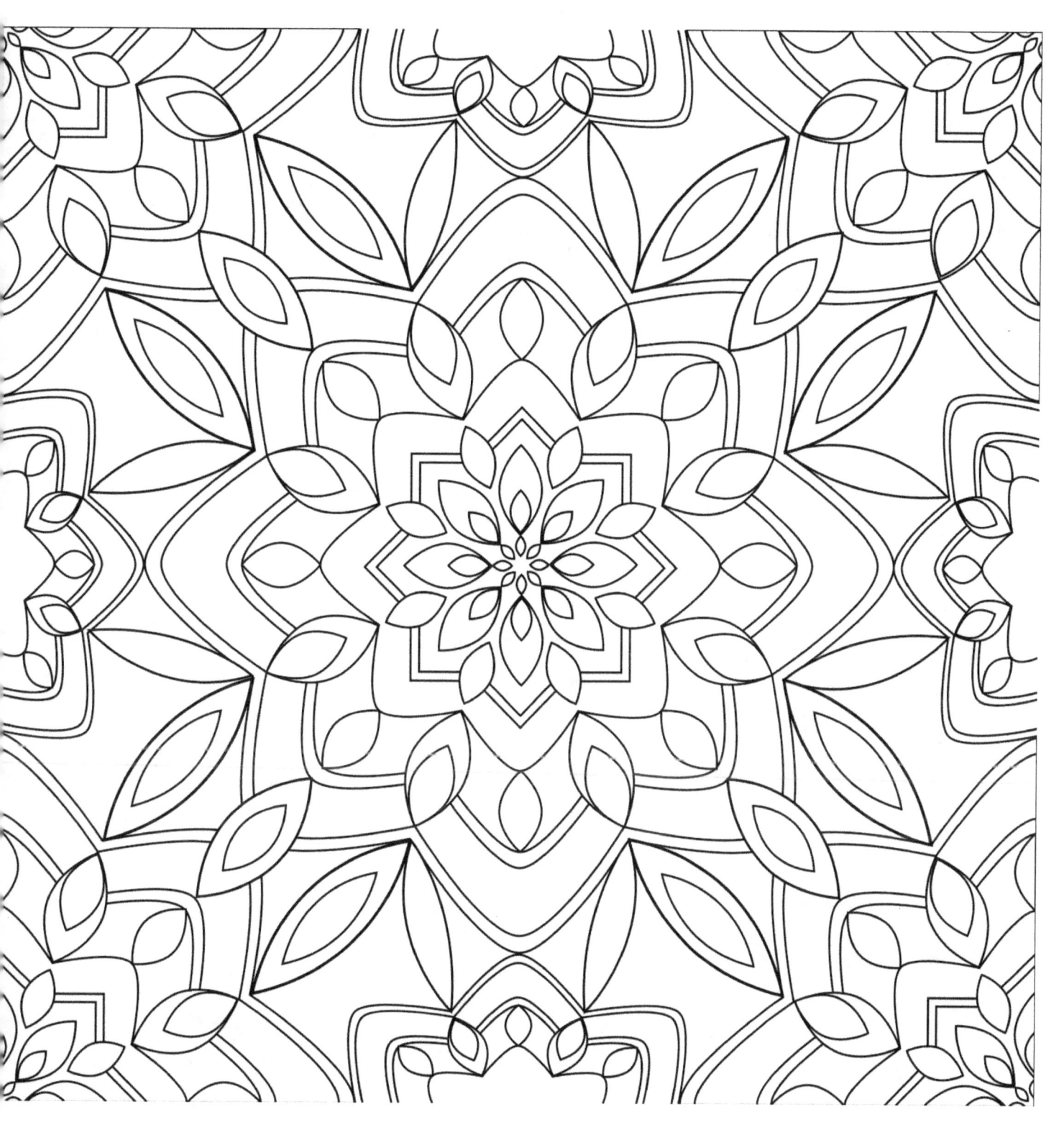

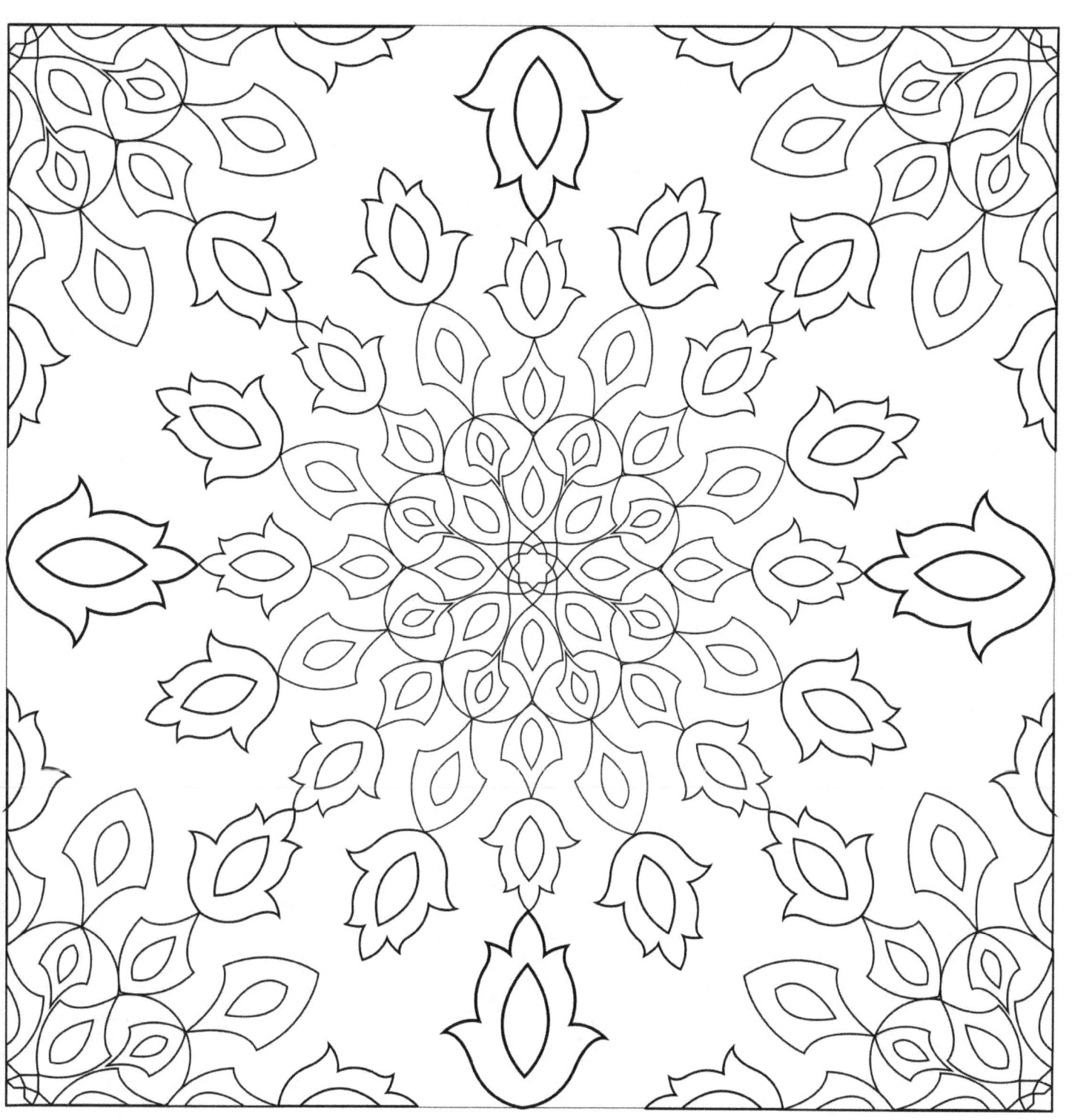

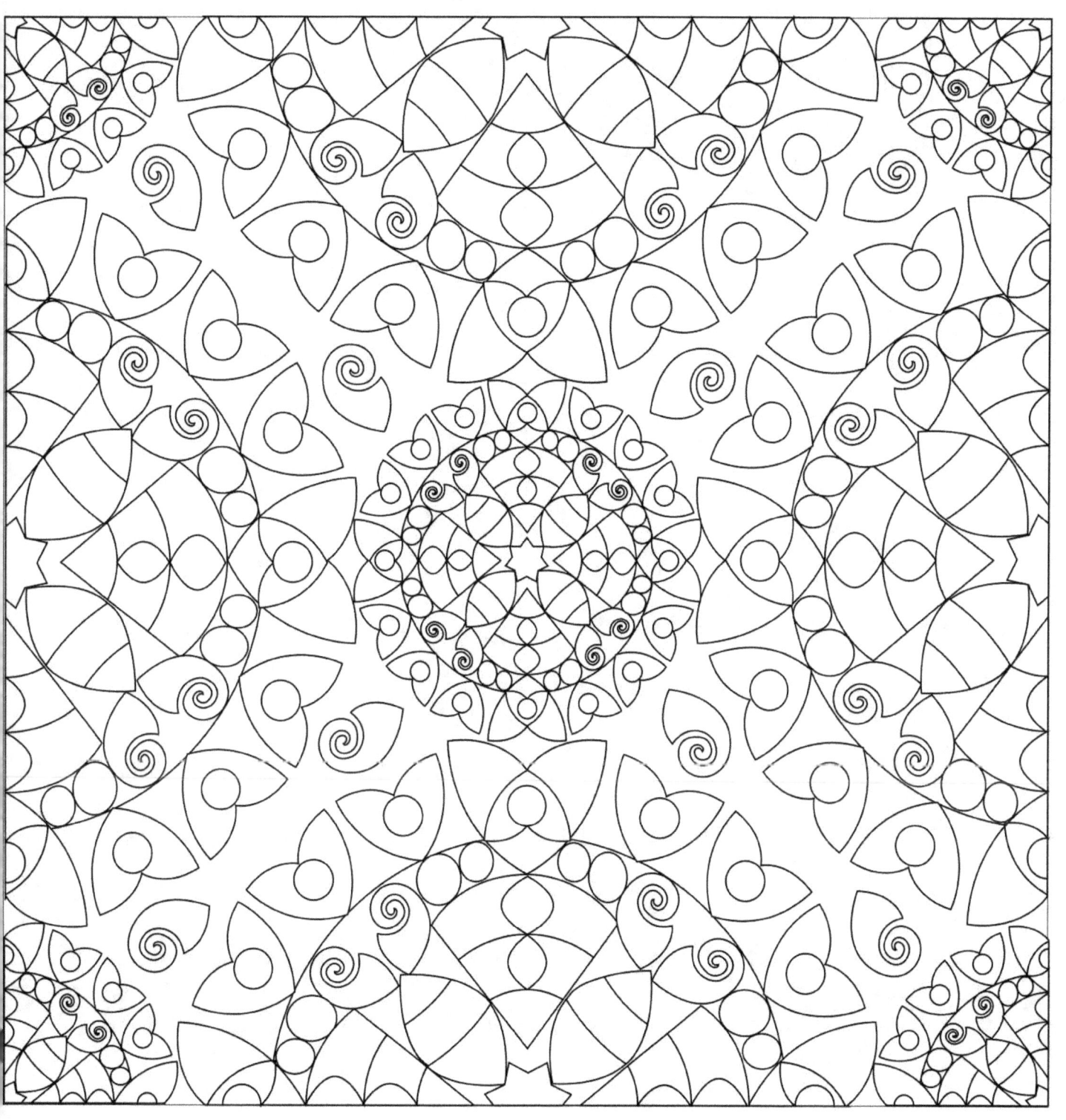

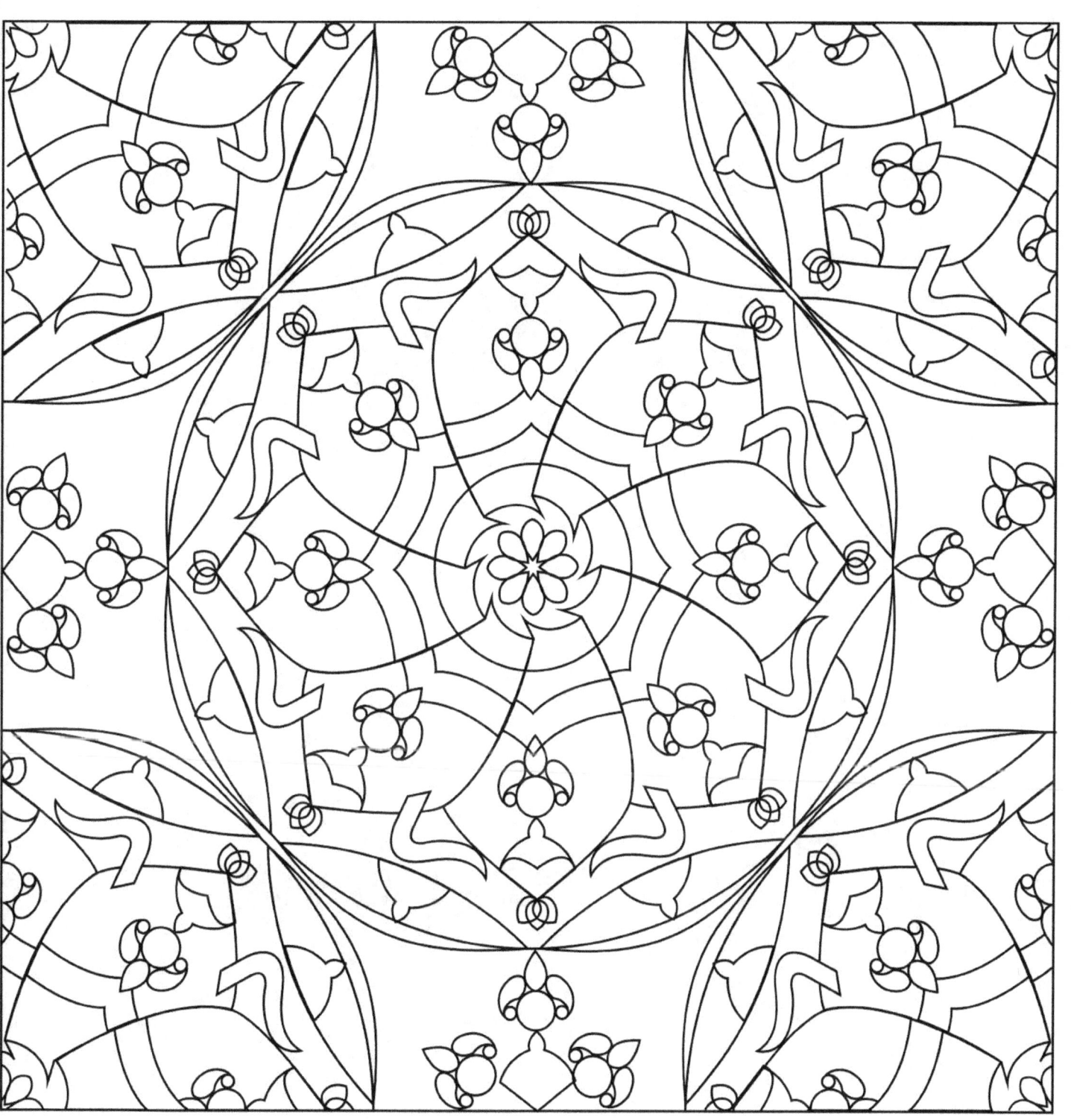

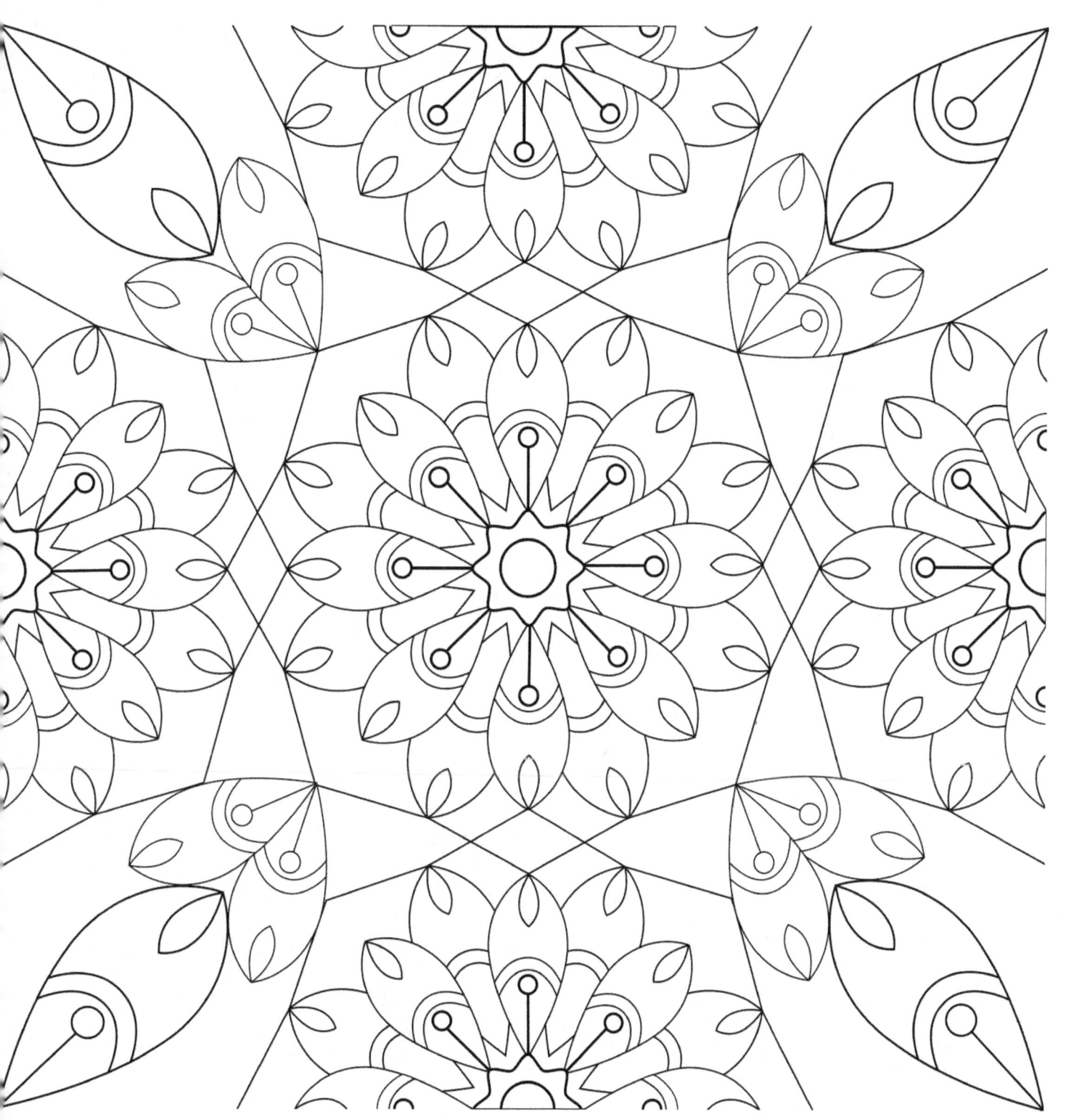

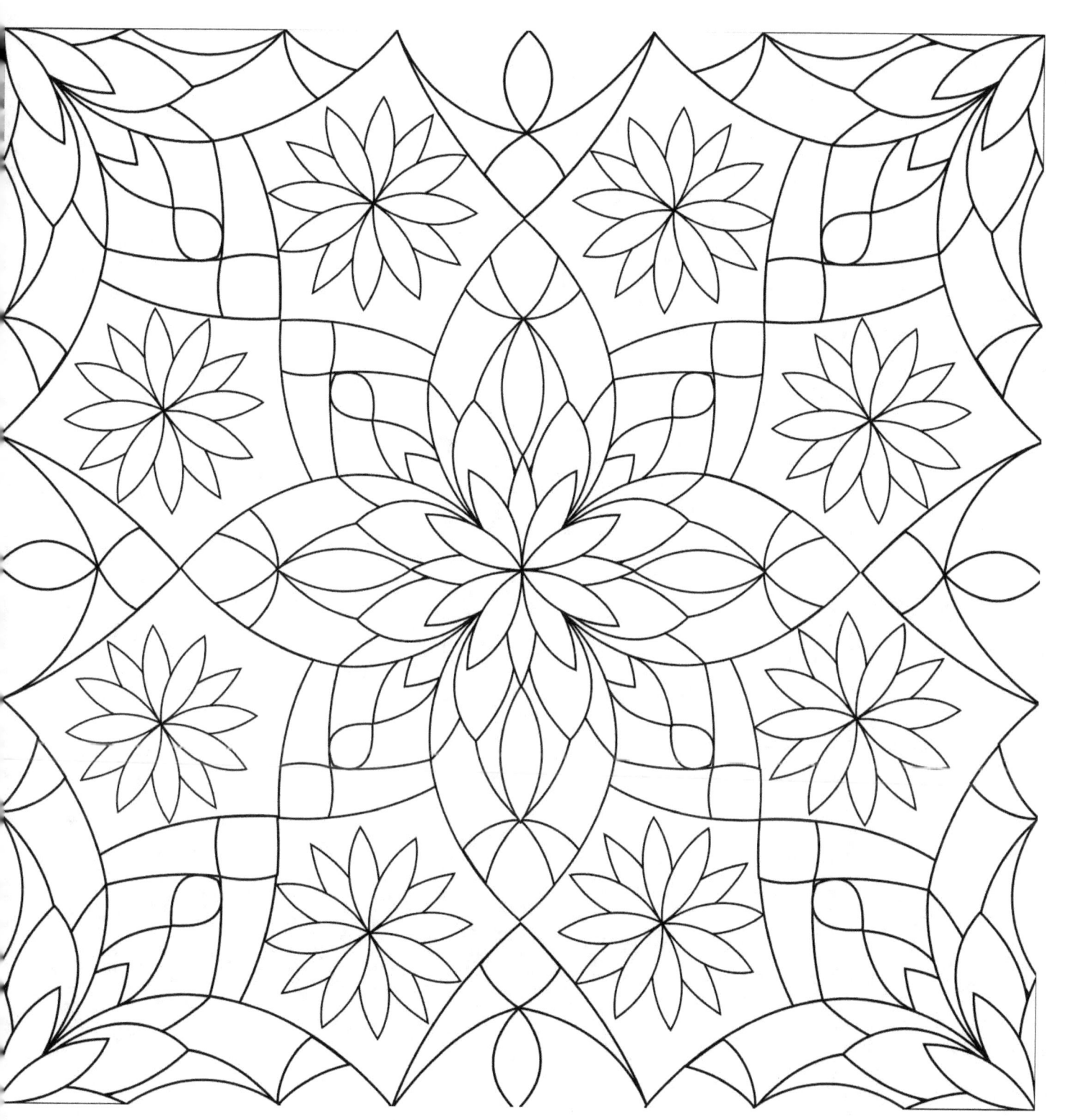

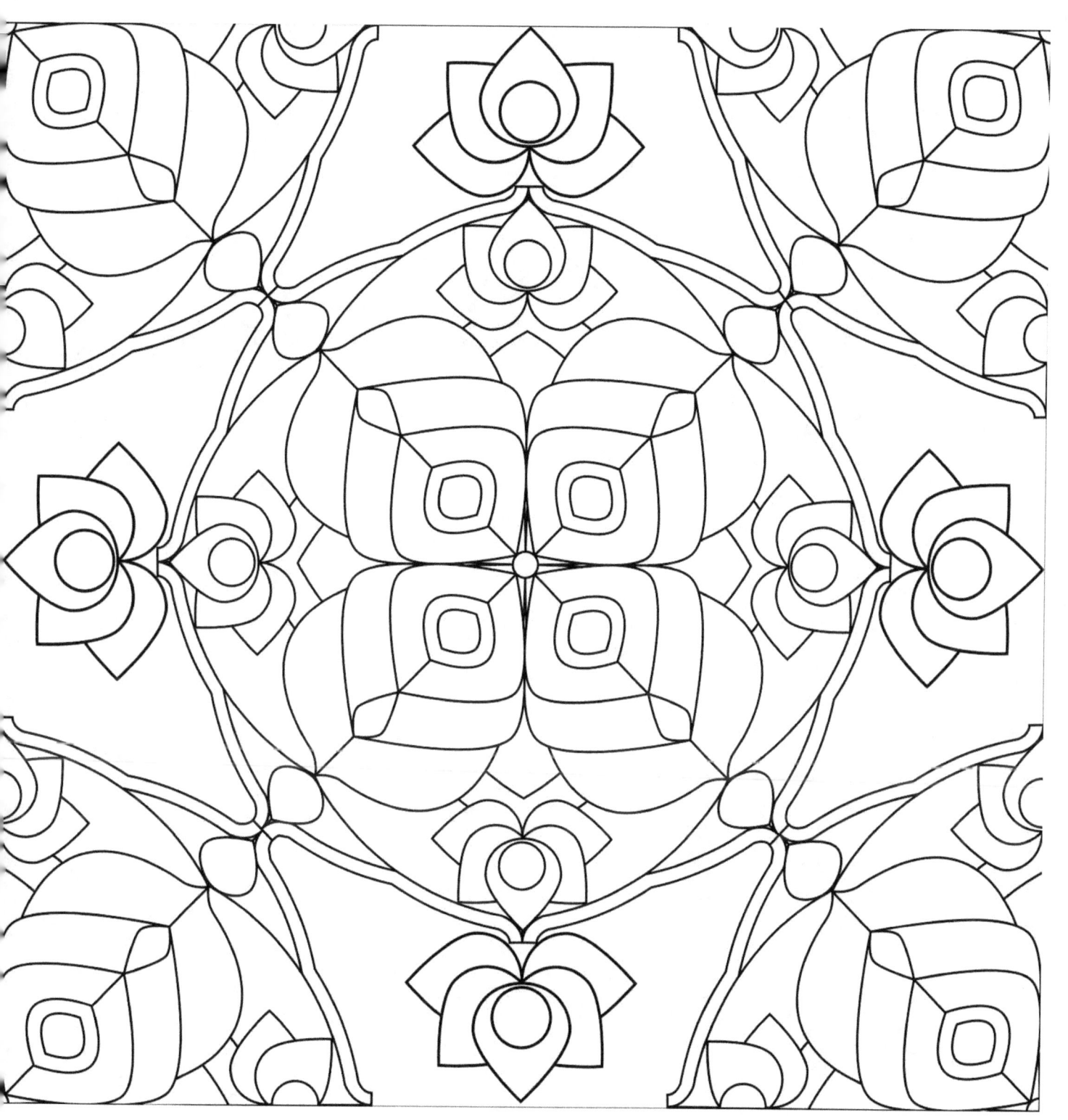

Thank You!

Thank you for purchasing Floral Mandala Art. It is the first volume in a series planned for release in the last few months of 2015. Please check at Amazon or Barnes & Noble for additional Volumes.

We would also love to see your creativity! Please share photos of your coloring pages on Amazon in the book review section, and on any social media sites you use. Follow us on Pinterest or at our main website to be the first to know when new content is published.

Pinterest - https://www.pinterest.com/eperceptions/

Website – http://www.ElectronicPerceptions.com

www.ingramcontent.com/pod-product-compliance
Lightning Source LLC
Chambersburg PA
CBHW081017170526
45158CB00010B/3077